Simple & Delicious

MUFFINS

Simple & Delicious

MUFFINS

OVER 100 SENSATIONAL RECIPES FOR MUFFIN LOVERS

This edition published in 2012
LOVE FOOD is an imprint of Parragon Books Ltd

Parragon
Chartist House
15–17 Trim Street
Bath, BA1 1HA, UK

ISBN: 978-1-78186-776-1

Printed in China

Cover design by Geoff Borin

Notes for the Reader
This book uses both metric and imperial measurements. Follow the same units of measurement throughout; do not mix metric and imperial. All spoon measurements are level: teaspoons are assumed to be 5 ml, and tablespoons are assumed to be 15 ml. Unless otherwise stated, milk is assumed to be full fat, eggs and individual vegetables are medium, and pepper is freshly ground black pepper. Unless otherwise stated, all root vegetables should be washed in plain water and peeled prior to using.

For best results, use a food thermometer when cooking meat and poultry – check the latest government guidelines for current advice.

Garnishes, decorations and serving suggestions are all optional and not necessarily included in the recipe ingredients or method.

The times given are an approximate guide only. Preparation times differ according to the techniques used by different people and the cooking times may also vary from those given. Optional ingredients, variations or serving suggestions have not been included in the time calculations.

Recipes using raw or very lightly cooked eggs should be avoided by infants, the elderly, pregnant women, convalescents and anyone suffering from an illness. Pregnant and breastfeeding women are advised to avoid eating peanuts and peanut products. Sufferers from nut allergies should be aware that some of the ready-made ingredients used in the recipes in this book may contain nuts. Always check the packaging before use.

Vegetarians should be aware that some of the ready-made ingredients used in the recipes in this book may contain animal products. Always check the packaging before use.

Contents

Introduction

There's something so satisfying about baking a batch of muffins. Perhaps it's because they're so simple to make, or because there are so many delicious variations, from fresh fruit to chocolate, or simply because they look and smell so wonderfully appetizing. Even so, the pleasure of making them is secondary to the sheer bliss of biting into the still warm, melt-in-the-mouth texture of a freshly baked muffin.

Everybody loves the comforting smell of muffins baking in the kitchen. They are satisfyingly quick and easy to make, and their light, fresh texture and distinctive flavour make them completely irresistible to all. Muffins are perfect as an after-school snack or a mid-morning indulgence, and will always be popular as a treat to offer friends and family.

For picnics or packed lunches, muffins are ideal as they are easily transportable and incredibly versatile. They can also be used as an alternative to baking a large cake for celebrations and special occasions. For a birthday, wedding or anniversary try baking a fresh batch of muffins and decorate to suit – they will be sure to impress! Savoury muffins are great for a Saturday morning brunch or as an accompaniment to soup on a cold winter's day. For a drinks party bake savoury muffins in mini muffin cups for an unusual canapé.

Useful equipment

Having the right equipment is essential to creating perfect muffins, but you don't need a kitchen full of fancy utensils. A large bowl, sieve, jug, spoon, set of scales and set of measuring spoons are all that's needed to make most muffins.

For the tin, choose one that has rounded corners and seamless cups. Non-stick surfaces are available, as are silicone muffin moulds (which are also non-stick). A standard-size muffin tin has 6 or 12 cup-shaped depressions, whilst jumbo-size muffin tins have 6 depressions and mini-size tins usually 12 or 24 depressions.

Muffins can be baked directly in the tin or in paper muffin cases. When baking directly in the tin it is important to grease the tin generously with oil or melted butter for easy removal. It is best to bake savoury muffins directly in the tin so that they have a crust. Paper muffin cases, available in several sizes, can be placed inside the depressions in the muffin tin and will prevent any difficulties in getting the muffins out of the tin. Paper cases also help to keep the muffins moist and make transporting them for a picnic or packed lunch easy.

All the instructions you will need are included in the recipes so, provided you follow them carefully, you really cannot go wrong. Nevertheless, the following hints and tips should be beneficial for both beginners and more experienced cooks and will help to ensure perfect results every time.

- Always preheat the oven and read the recipe carefully before cooking.
- When baking muffins, try to resist the temptation to open the oven door during the first half of the cooking time as cold air can cause the mixture to sink in the middle.
- It is important that ingredients are measured accurately, so it is worth investing in good-quality scales and standard measuring spoons.
- After adding the flour to the muffin mixture, do not overbeat it because this will make the mixture tough.
- Don't be tempted to add more baking powder, thinking the muffins will rise more. Too much will cause them to over-rise and then collapse and the muffins will be heavy. They will also taste unpleasant.
- Once you've made the mixture, bake it immediately as, when the liquid has been added to the flour, the baking powder starts to work by relaxing the dough and allowing it to rise.
- Don't over-bake the muffins as they will become dry. For even browning, position the muffins on the middle rack of the oven.
- Use a wire rack for cooling muffins to ensure that any excess steam can escape without making the muffins soggy. If you don't have a wire rack, use the rack from a grill pan or a barbecue rack.
- Muffins are best eaten freshly baked or at least on the day they are made but, if necessary, can be stored in an airtight tin.

- Ideally, store muffins undecorated. Icing, sauces and any other decorations can be added before serving. To reheat, place in the oven at 150°C/300°F/Gas Mark 2 for 5–10 minutes or in the microwave on HIGH for 20–30 seconds.
- Muffins are perfect for freezing. Thaw at room temperature for 2–3 hours or reheat frozen muffins on a baking tray at 180°C/350°F/Gas Mark 4 for 15–20 minutes.

Finally, when serving your muffins, presentation makes all the difference. Serve the delicate types on fine china or glass plates or for a casual gathering with family and friends serve muffins on a pretty plate with a colourful napkin, and for savoury lunchtime muffins use a basket or wooden board. The beautifully photographed recipes in this book will capture your imagination!

1

Fruit & Nut

Blueberry Muffins

makes 12

oil or melted butter,
for greasing (if using)

280 g/10 oz plain flour

1 tbsp baking powder

pinch of salt

115 g/4 oz soft light brown
sugar

150 g/5½ oz frozen
blueberries

2 eggs

250 ml/9 fl oz milk

85 g/3 oz butter, melted
and cooled

1 tsp vanilla extract

finely grated rind of
1 lemon

Preheat the oven to 200°C/400°F/Gas Mark 6. Grease a 12-cup muffin tin or line with 12 paper cases. Sift together the flour, baking powder and salt into a large bowl. Stir in the sugar and blueberries.

Lightly beat the eggs in a large bowl then beat in the milk, butter, vanilla extract and lemon rind. Make a well in the centre of the dry ingredients and pour in the beaten liquid ingredients. Stir gently until just combined; do not over-mix.

Spoon the mixture into the prepared muffin tin. Bake in the preheated oven for about 20 minutes until well risen, golden brown and firm to the touch.

Leave the muffins in the tin for 5 minutes then serve warm or transfer to a wire rack and leave to cool.

Raspberry Crumble Muffins

makes 12

oil or melted butter,
for greasing (if using)

280 g/10 oz plain flour

1 tbsp baking powder

½ tsp bicarbonate of soda

pinch of salt

115 g/4 oz caster sugar

2 eggs

250 ml/9 fl oz natural
yogurt

85 g/3 oz butter, melted
and cooled

1 tsp vanilla extract

150 g/5½ oz frozen
raspberries

crumble topping

50 g/1¾ oz plain flour

35 g/1¼ oz butter

25 g/1 oz caster sugar

Preheat the oven to 200°C/400°F/Gas Mark 6. Grease a 12-cup muffin tin or line with 12 paper cases.

To make the crumble topping, sift the flour into a bowl. Cut the butter into small pieces, add to the bowl with the flour and rub it in with your fingertips until the mixture resembles fine breadcrumbs. Stir in the sugar and set aside.

To make the muffins, sift together the flour, baking powder, bicarbonate of soda and salt into a large bowl. Stir in the sugar.

Lightly beat the eggs in a large bowl then beat in the yogurt, butter and vanilla extract. Make a well in the centre of the dry ingredients, pour in the beaten liquid ingredients and add the raspberries. Stir gently until just combined; do not over-mix.

Spoon the mixture into the prepared muffin tin. Scatter the crumble topping over each muffin and press down lightly. Bake in the preheated oven for about 20 minutes until well risen, golden brown and firm to the touch.

Leave the muffins in the tin for 5 minutes then serve warm or transfer to a wire rack and leave to cool.

Lemon & Poppy Seed Muffins

makes 12

oil or melted butter,
for greasing (if using)

280 g/10 oz plain flour

1 tbsp baking powder

pinch of salt

115 g/4 oz caster sugar

2 tbsp poppy seeds

2 eggs

250 ml/9 fl oz milk

85 g/3 oz butter, melted
and cooled

finely grated rind of
2 lemons

Preheat the oven to 200°C/400°F/Gas Mark 6. Grease a 12-cup muffin tin or line with 12 paper cases. Sift together the flour, baking powder and salt into a large bowl. Stir in the sugar and poppy seeds.

Lightly beat the eggs in a large bowl then beat in the milk, butter and lemon rind. Make a well in the centre of the dry ingredients and pour in the beaten liquid ingredients. Stir gently until just combined; do not over-mix.

Spoon the mixture into the prepared muffin tin. Bake in the preheated oven for about 20 minutes until well risen, golden brown and firm to the touch.

Leave the muffins in the tin for 5 minutes then serve warm or transfer to a wire rack and leave to cool.

Cranberry Muffins

makes 10

oil or melted butter,
for greasing (if using)

175 g/6 oz self-raising flour

55 g/2 oz self-raising
wholemeal flour

1 tsp ground cinnamon

½ tsp bicarbonate of soda

1 egg, beaten

70 g/2½ oz thin-cut orange
marmalade

150 ml/5 fl oz skimmed or
semi-skimmed milk

5 tbsp corn oil

115 g/4 oz peeled,
cored and finely diced
eating apple

115 g/4 oz fresh or frozen
cranberries, thawed
if frozen

1 tbsp rolled oats

Preheat the oven to 200°C/400°F/Gas Mark 6. Grease 10 cups of a 12-cup muffin tin or line with 10 paper cases. Sift together the flours, cinnamon and bicarbonate of soda into a large bowl and combine thoroughly.

Blend the egg with the marmalade in a large bowl, then beat the milk and oil into the egg mixture. Make a well in the centre of the dry ingredients and pour in the beaten liquid ingredients. Stir gently until just combined; do not over-mix. Quickly stir in the apple and cranberries.

Spoon the mixture into the prepared muffin tin and sprinkle a few oats over each muffin. Bake in the preheated oven for about 20 minutes until well risen, golden brown and firm to the touch.

Leave the muffins in the tin for 5 minutes then serve warm or transfer to a wire rack and leave to cool.

Apple Streusel Muffins

makes 12

oil or melted butter, for greasing (if using)

280 g/10 oz plain flour

1 tbsp baking powder

½ tsp ground cinnamon

pinch of salt

115 g/4 oz soft light brown sugar

1 large cooking apple, peeled, cored and finely chopped

2 eggs

250 ml/9 fl oz milk

85 g/3 oz butter, melted and cooled

streusel topping

50 g/1¾ oz plain white flour

¼ tsp ground cinnamon

35 g/1¼ oz butter

25 g/1 oz soft light brown sugar

Preheat the oven to 200°C/400°F/Gas Mark 6. Grease a 12-cup muffin tin or line with 12 paper cases.

To make the streusel topping, sift together the flour and cinnamon into a large bowl. Cut the butter into small pieces, add to the bowl with the flour and rub it in with your fingertips until the mixture resembles fine breadcrumbs. Stir in the sugar and set aside.

To make the muffins, sift together the flour, baking powder, cinnamon and salt into a large bowl. Stir in the sugar. Add the apple to the flour mixture and stir together.

Lightly beat the eggs in a large bowl then beat in the milk and butter. Make a well in the centre of the dry ingredients and pour in the beaten liquid ingredients. Stir gently until just combined; do not over-mix.

Spoon the mixture into the prepared muffin tin. Scatter the streusel topping over each muffin. Bake in the preheated oven for about 20 minutes until well risen, golden brown and firm to the touch.

Leave the muffins in the tin for 5 minutes then serve warm or transfer to a wire rack and leave to cool.

Fruity Muffins

makes 10

oil or melted butter,
for greasing (if using)

280 g/10 oz self-raising
wholemeal flour

2 tsp baking powder

2 tbsp dark muscovado
sugar

100 g/3½ oz ready-to-eat
dried apricots, finely
chopped

1 banana, mashed with
1 tbsp orange juice

1 tsp finely grated
orange rind

300 ml/10 fl oz skimmed
milk

1 egg, beaten

3 tbsp sunflower oil

2 tbsp rolled oats

Preheat the oven to 200°C/400°F/Gas Mark 6. Grease 10 cups of a 12-cup muffin tin or line with 10 paper cases. Sift together the flour and baking powder into a large bowl and combine thoroughly, adding any husks that remain in the sieve. Stir in the sugar and chopped apricots.

Blend the banana and orange rind with the milk, egg and oil in a large bowl. Make a well in the centre of the dry ingredients and pour in the beaten liquid ingredients. Stir gently until just combined; do not over-mix.

Spoon the mixture into the prepared muffin tin and sprinkle a few oats over each muffin. Bake in the preheated oven for 25–30 minutes until well risen, golden brown and firm to the touch.

Leave the muffins in the tin for 5 minutes then serve warm or transfer to a wire rack and leave to cool.

Honey & Lemon Muffins

makes 12

oil or melted butter,
for greasing (if using)

50 g/1¾ oz caster sugar

2 tbsp butter, melted and
cooled

150 ml/5 fl oz buttermilk

2 eggs, beaten

4 tbsp flower honey

finely grated rind of
1 lemon

225 g/8 oz plain flour

150 g/5½ oz oat bran

1½ tbsp baking powder

juice of ½ lemon

Preheat the oven to 180°C/350°F/Gas Mark 4. Grease a 12-cup muffin tin or line with 12 paper cases. Put the sugar into a jug and add the butter, buttermilk, eggs, half the honey and the lemon rind. Briefly mix to combine.

Sift the flour into a large bowl, add the oat bran and baking powder, and stir to combine. Make a well in the centre of the dry ingredients and pour in the beaten liquid ingredients.

Spoon the mixture into the prepared muffin tin. Bake in the preheated oven for 25 minutes until well risen, golden brown and firm to the touch.

Mix the lemon juice with the remaining honey in a small bowl or jug and drizzle over the muffins while they are still hot. Let the muffins stand for 10 minutes before serving.

Toasted Almond & Apricot Muffins

makes 12

100 g/3½ oz dried apricots

3 tbsp fresh orange juice

oil or melted butter,
for greasing (if using)

50 g/1¾ oz blanched
almonds

280 g/10 oz plain flour

1 tbsp baking powder

pinch of salt

115 g/4 oz caster sugar

2 eggs

200 ml/7 fl oz buttermilk

85 g/3 oz butter, melted
and cooled

¼ tsp almond essence

40 g/1½ oz flaked almonds

Cut the apricots into small pieces and put in a bowl. Add the orange juice and leave to soak for 1 hour. Grease a 12-cup muffin tin or line with 12 paper cases.

Meanwhile, line a grill pan with a sheet of foil and spread out the almonds. Toast under the grill until golden brown, turning frequently. When cool enough to handle, coarsely chop the almonds.

Preheat the oven to 200°C/400°F/Gas Mark 6. Sift together the flour, baking powder and salt into a large bowl. Stir in the sugar and chopped almonds.

Lightly beat the eggs in a large bowl then beat in the buttermilk, butter and almond essence. Make a well in the centre of the dry ingredients, pour in the beaten liquid ingredients and add the soaked, drained apricots. Stir gently until just combined; do not over-mix.

Spoon the mixture into the prepared muffin tin. Scatter a few flaked almonds on top of each muffin. Bake in the preheated oven for about 20 minutes until well risen, golden brown and firm to the touch.

Leave the muffins in the tin for 5 minutes then serve warm or transfer to a wire rack and leave to cool.

Wheatgerm, Banana & Pumpkin Seed Muffins

makes 12

oil or melted butter,
for greasing (if using)

140 g/5 oz plain flour

1 tbsp baking powder

115 g/4 oz caster sugar

140 g/5 oz wheatgerm

85 g/3 oz pumpkin seeds

2 bananas

about 150 ml/5 fl oz
skimmed milk

2 eggs

6 tbsp sunflower oil

Preheat the oven to 200°C/400°F/Gas Mark 6. Grease a 12-cup muffin tin or line with 12 paper cases. Sift together the flour and baking powder into a large bowl. Stir in the sugar, wheatgerm and 50 g/1¾ oz of the pumpkin seeds.

Mash the bananas in a large bowl. Make up the purée to 250 ml/9 fl oz with milk.

Lightly beat the eggs in a large bowl then beat in the banana and milk mixture and the oil. Make a well in the centre of the dry ingredients and pour in the beaten liquid ingredients. Stir gently until just combined; do not over-mix.

Spoon the mixture into the prepared muffin tin. Sprinkle the remaining pumpkin seeds over the tops of the muffins. Bake in the preheated oven for about 20 minutes until well risen, golden brown and firm to the touch.

Leave the muffins in the tin for 5 minutes then serve warm or transfer to a wire rack and leave to cool.

Oaty Apple & Cinnamon Muffins

makes 12

oil or melted butter,
for greasing (if using)

200 g/7 oz wholemeal
plain flour

75 g/2¾ oz fine oatmeal

2 tsp baking powder

125 g/4½ oz soft light
brown sugar

2 large eggs

225 ml/8 fl oz
semi-skimmed milk

100 ml/3½ fl oz groundnut
oil

1 tsp vanilla extract

1 tsp ground cinnamon

1 large cooking apple,
peeled, cored and grated

Preheat the oven to 180°C/350°F/Gas Mark 4. Grease a 12-cup muffin tin or line with 12 paper cases.

Sift together the flour, oatmeal and baking powder into a large bowl, adding any husks that remain. Stir in the sugar.

Lightly beat the eggs in a large bowl then beat in the milk and oil. Make a well in the centre of the dry ingredients and pour in the beaten liquid ingredients. Add the vanilla extract and cinnamon and stir gently until just combined; do not over-mix.

Stir the apple into the mixture. Spoon the mixture into the prepared muffin tin. Bake in the preheated oven for 20–25 minutes until well risen, golden brown and firm to the touch.

Leave the muffins in the tin for 5 minutes then serve warm or transfer to a wire rack and leave to cool.

Rhubarb, Raisin & Ginger Muffins

makes 12

oil or melted butter, for greasing (if using)

250 g/9 oz rhubarb

200 g/7 oz plain flour

2 tsp baking powder

115 g/4 oz caster sugar

125 g/4½ oz butter, melted and cooled

100 ml/3½ fl oz milk

2 eggs, lightly beaten

3 tbsp raisins

3 pieces stem ginger, chopped

Preheat the oven to 180°C/350°F/Gas Mark 4. Grease a 12-cup muffin tin or line with 12 paper cases. Chop the rhubarb into lengths of about 1 cm/½ inch.

Sift together the flour and baking powder into a large bowl. Stir in the sugar. Pour the melted butter and milk in a large bowl and beat in the eggs. Make a well in the centre of the dry ingredients and pour in the beaten liquid ingredients. Gently stir in the rhubarb, raisins and stem ginger.

Spoon the mixture into the prepared muffin tin. Bake in the preheated oven for 15–20 minutes until well risen, golden brown and firm to the touch.

Leave the muffins in the tin for 5 minutes then serve warm or transfer to a wire rack and leave to cool.

Apple & Raspberry Muffins

makes 12

3 large cooking apples, peeled and cored

450 ml/16 fl oz water

1½ tsp allspice

oil or melted butter, for greasing (if using)

300 g/10½ oz plain wholemeal flour

1 tbsp baking powder

¼ tsp salt

3 tbsp caster sugar

85 g/3 oz fresh raspberries

Thinly slice 2 of the apples and place them in a saucepan with 6 tablespoons of the water. Bring to the boil, then reduce the heat. Stir in ½ teaspoon of the allspice, cover the pan and simmer, stirring occasionally, for 15–20 minutes or until the water has been absorbed. Remove from the heat and cool. Blend in a food processor until smooth. Stir in the remaining water and mix well.

Grease a 12-cup muffin tin or line with 12 paper cases. Sift together the flour, baking powder, salt and remaining allspice in a large bowl. Stir in the sugar.

Chop the remaining apple and add to the flour mixture. Add the raspberries, then combine gently with the flour mixture until lightly coated. Finally, add in the cooled apple and water mixture and stir gently until just combined; do not over-mix.

Spoon the mixture into the prepared muffin tin. Bake in the preheated oven for 25 minutes until well risen, golden brown and firm to the touch.

Leave the muffins in the tin for 5 minutes then serve warm or transfer to a wire rack and leave to cool.

Dried Cherry Cheesecake Muffins

makes 12

oil or melted butter,
for greasing (if using)

200 g/7 oz cream cheese

150 g/5½ oz caster sugar

3 large eggs, lightly beaten

150 g/5½ oz butter, melted
and cooled

300 g/10½ oz self-raising
flour

100 g/3½ oz dried cherries,
chopped

Preheat the oven to 180°C/350°F/Gas Mark 4. Grease a 12-cup muffin tin or line with 12 paper cases.

In a large bowl, whisk the cream cheese and sugar together, adding the eggs one at a time until well combined, and then stir in the melted butter.

Sift the flour into a large bowl and stir in the cherries. Make a well in the centre of the dry ingredients and pour in the beaten liquid ingredients. Gently stir until just combined; do not over-mix.

Spoon the mixture into the prepared muffin tin. Bake in the preheated oven for 12–15 minutes until well risen, golden brown and firm to the touch.

Leave the muffins in the tin for 5 minutes then serve warm or transfer to a wire rack and leave to cool.

Strawberry Explosion Muffins

makes 12

oil or melted butter,
for greasing (if using)

225 g/8 oz plain flour

1 tsp baking powder

140 g/5 oz golden caster
sugar

100 ml/3½ fl oz milk

2 large eggs

140 g/5 oz butter, melted
and cooled

12 tsp strawberry jam

icing

45 g/1½ oz butter, softened

85 g/3 oz icing sugar

½ tsp vanilla extract

1–2 tsp milk

6 strawberries, halved,
to decorate

Preheat the oven to 180°C/350°F/Gas Mark 4. Grease a 12-cup muffin tin or line with 12 paper cases. Sift together the flour and baking powder into a large bowl. Stir in the caster sugar.

Pour the milk, eggs and melted butter in a large bowl and beat together. Make a well in the centre of the dry ingredients and pour in the beaten liquid ingredients. Stir gently until just combined; do not over-mix.

Spoon a heaped dessertspoon of the mixture into each of the prepared cups or cases, then add a teaspoonful of jam. Top with the rest of the muffin mixture. Bake in the preheated oven for 20–25 minutes until well risen, golden brown and firm to the touch. Leave the muffins in the tin for 5 minutes then transfer to a wire rack and leave to cool.

To make the icing, beat together the butter, icing sugar, vanilla extract and milk in a small bowl until smooth and creamy.

Place a spoonful of the icing on top of each muffin, then decorate with a strawberry half.

Nectarine & Banana Muffins

makes 12

oil or melted butter, for greasing (if using)

250 g/9 oz plain flour

1 tsp bicarbonate of soda

¼ tsp salt

¼ tsp allspice

100 g/3½ oz caster sugar

55 g/2 oz shelled almonds, chopped

175 g/6 oz ripe nectarine, peeled and chopped

1 ripe banana, sliced

2 large eggs

75 ml/2½ fl oz sunflower or peanut oil

75 ml/2½ fl oz thick natural or banana-flavoured yogurt

1 tsp almond essence

Preheat the oven to 200°C/400°F/Gas Mark 6. Grease a 12-cup muffin tin or line with 12 paper cases. Sift together the flour, bicarbonate of soda, salt and allspice into a large bowl. Add the sugar and chopped almonds and stir together.

In a separate large bowl, mash the nectarine and banana together, then stir in the eggs, sunflower oil, yogurt and almond essence. Make a well in the centre of the dry ingredients and pour in the liquid ingredients. Stir gently until just combined; do not over-mix.

Spoon the mixture into the prepared muffin tin. Bake in the preheated oven for 20 minutes until well risen, golden brown and firm to the touch.

Leave the muffins in the tin for 5 minutes then serve warm or transfer to a wire rack and leave to cool.

Walnut & Cinnamon Muffins

makes 12

oil or melted butter,
for greasing (if using)

280 g/10 oz plain flour

1 tbsp baking powder

1 tsp ground cinnamon

pinch of salt

115 g/4 oz soft light brown
sugar

100 g/3½ oz walnuts,
coarsely chopped

2 eggs

250 ml/9 fl oz milk

85 g/3 oz butter, melted
and cooled

1 tsp vanilla extract

Preheat the oven to 200°C/400°F/Gas Mark 6. Grease a 12-cup muffin tin or line with 12 paper cases. Sift together the flour, baking powder, cinnamon and salt into a large bowl. Stir in the sugar and walnuts.

Lightly beat the eggs in a large bowl then beat in the milk, butter and vanilla extract. Make a well in the centre of the dry ingredients and pour in the beaten liquid ingredients. Stir gently until just combined; do not over-mix.

Spoon the mixture into the prepared muffin tin. Bake in the preheated oven for about 20 minutes until well risen, golden brown and firm to the touch.

Leave the muffins in the tin for 5 minutes then serve warm or transfer to a wire rack and leave to cool.

Fig & Almond Muffins

makes 12

oil or melted butter, for greasing (if using)

250 g/9 oz plain flour

1 tsp bicarbonate of soda

½ tsp salt

225 g/8 oz demerara sugar

85 g/3 oz dried figs, chopped

115 g/4 oz almonds, chopped, plus extra to decorate

2 tbsp sunflower or peanut oil

200 ml/7 fl oz water

1 tsp almond essence

Preheat the oven to 190°C/375°F/Gas Mark 5. Grease a 12-cup muffin tin or line with 12 paper cases. Sift together the flour, bicarbonate of soda and salt into a large bowl. Add the sugar and stir together.

In a separate large bowl, mix together the figs, almonds and sunflower oil then stir in the water and almond essence. Make a well in the centre of the dry ingredients and pour in the liquid ingredients. Stir gently until just combined; do not over-mix.

Spoon the mixture into the prepared muffin tin. Sprinkle the remaining almonds on top of the muffins. Bake in the preheated oven for 25 minutes until well risen, golden brown and firm to the touch.

Leave the muffins in the tin for 5 minutes then serve warm or transfer to a wire rack and leave to cool.

Fudge Nut Muffins

makes 12

oil or melted butter,
for greasing (if using)

250 g/9 oz plain flour

4 tsp baking powder

85 g/3 oz caster sugar

6 tbsp crunchy peanut
butter

1 large egg, beaten

4 tbsp butter, melted and
cooled

175 ml/6 fl oz milk

150 g/5½ oz vanilla fudge,
cut into small pieces

3 tbsp roughly chopped
unsalted peanuts

Preheat the oven to 200°C/400°F/Gas Mark 6. Grease a 12-cup muffin tin or line with 12 paper cases. Sift together the flour and baking powder into a large bowl. Stir in the sugar. Add the peanut butter and stir until the mixture resembles breadcrumbs.

Beat together the egg, butter and milk in a large bowl until blended. Make a well in the centre of the dry ingredients and pour in the beaten liquid ingredients. Lightly stir in the fudge pieces. Stir gently until just combined; do not over-mix.

Spoon the mixture into the prepared muffin tin. Sprinkle the peanuts on top of the muffins. Bake in the preheated oven for 20–25 minutes until well risen, golden brown and firm to the touch.

Leave the muffins in the tin for 5 minutes then serve warm or transfer to a wire rack and leave to cool.

2

Chocolate

Chocolate Chunk Muffins

makes 12

oil or melted butter,
for greasing (if using)

280 g/10 oz plain flour

1 tbsp baking powder

pinch of salt

115 g/4 oz caster sugar

175 g/6 oz chocolate
chunks

2 eggs

250 ml/9 fl oz milk

85 g/3 oz butter, melted
and cooled

1 tsp vanilla extract

Preheat the oven to 200°C/400°F/Gas Mark 6. Grease a 12-cup muffin tin or line with 12 paper cases. Sift together the flour, baking powder and salt into a large bowl. Stir in the sugar and chocolate chunks.

Lightly beat the eggs in a large bowl then beat in the milk, butter and vanilla extract.

Make a well in the centre of the dry ingredients and pour in the beaten liquid ingredients. Stir gently until just combined; do not over-mix.

Spoon the mixture into the prepared muffin tin. Bake in the preheated oven for about 20 minutes until well risen, golden brown and firm to the touch.

Leave the muffins in the tin for 5 minutes then serve warm or transfer to a wire rack and leave to cool.

Mocha Muffins

makes 12

oil or melted butter,
for greasing (if using)

225 g/8 oz plain flour

1 tbsp baking powder

2 tbsp cocoa powder

pinch of salt

115 g/4 oz butter, melted
and cooled

150 g/5½ oz demerara
sugar

1 large egg, lightly beaten

125 ml/4 fl oz milk

1 tsp almond essence

2 tbsp strong coffee

1 tbsp instant coffee
powder

55 g/2 oz plain chocolate
chips

25 g/1 oz raisins

cocoa topping

3 tbsp demerara sugar

1 tbsp cocoa powder

1 tsp allspice

Preheat the oven to 190°C/375°F/Gas Mark 5. Grease a 12-cup muffin tin or line with 12 paper cases. Sift together the flour, baking powder, cocoa powder and salt into a large bowl.

Place the butter and demerara sugar in a separate large bowl and beat together until light and fluffy, then stir in the egg. Pour in the milk, almond essence and coffee, then add the coffee powder, chocolate chips and raisins and gently mix together.

Add the raisin mixture to the flour mixture. Stir gently until just combined; do not over-mix. Spoon the mixture into the prepared muffin tin.

To make the cocoa topping, place the demerara sugar in a small bowl, add the cocoa powder and allspice and mix together well. Sprinkle the topping over the muffins.

Bake in the preheated oven for 20 minutes until well risen and firm to the touch.

Leave the muffins in the tin for 5 minutes then serve warm or transfer to a wire rack and leave to cool.

Chocolate Fudge Muffins

makes 12

oil or melted butter,
for greasing (if using)

225 g/8 oz plain flour

55 g/2 oz cocoa powder

1 tbsp baking powder

pinch of salt

115 g/4 oz soft light brown
sugar

2 eggs

200 ml/7 fl oz soured cream

85 g/3 oz butter, melted
and cooled

3 tbsp golden syrup

Preheat the oven to 200°C/400°F/Gas Mark 6. Grease a 12-cup muffin tin or line with 12 paper cases. Sift together the flour, cocoa powder, baking powder and salt into a large bowl. Stir in the sugar.

Lightly beat the eggs in a large bowl then beat in the soured cream, butter and golden syrup. Make a well in the centre of the dry ingredients and pour in the beaten liquid ingredients. Stir gently until just combined; do not over-mix.

Spoon the mixture into the prepared muffin tin. Bake in the preheated oven for about 20 minutes until well risen and firm to the touch.

Leave the muffins in the tin for 5 minutes then serve warm or transfer to a wire rack and leave to cool.

Pecan Brownie Muffins

makes 12

oil or melted butter,
for greasing (if using)

115 g/4 oz pecan nuts

100 g/3½ oz plain flour

175 g/6 oz caster sugar

¼ tsp salt

1 tbsp baking powder

225 g/8 oz butter

115 g/4 oz plain chocolate

4 eggs, lightly beaten

1 tsp vanilla extract

Preheat the oven to 200°C/400°F/Gas Mark 6. Grease a 12-cup muffin tin or line with 12 paper cases. Reserve 12 pecan halves and roughly chop the rest.

Sift together the flour, sugar, salt and baking powder into a large bowl and make a well in the centre. Melt the butter and chocolate in a small saucepan over a very low heat, stirring frequently. Add to the flour mixture and stir to mix evenly.

Add the eggs and vanilla extract. Stir gently until just combined; do not over-mix. Stir in the chopped pecan nuts.

Spoon the mixture into the prepared muffin tin and add a pecan half on top of each. Bake in the preheated oven for 20–25 minutes until well risen and firm to the touch.

Leave the muffins in the tin for 5 minutes then serve warm or transfer to a wire rack and leave to cool.

Malted Chocolate Muffins

makes 12

oil or melted butter, for greasing (if using)

150 g/5½ oz malted chocolate balls

225 g/8 oz plain flour

55 g/2 oz cocoa powder

1 tbsp baking powder

pinch of salt

115 g/4 oz soft light brown sugar

2 eggs

250 ml/9 fl oz buttermilk

85 g/3 oz butter, melted and cooled

icing

55 g/2 oz plain chocolate

115 g/4 oz butter, softened

225 g/8 oz icing sugar

Preheat the oven to 200°C/400°F/Gas Mark 6. Grease a 12-cup muffin tin or line with 12 paper cases. Roughly crush the chocolate balls, reserving 12 whole ones to decorate.

Sift together the flour, cocoa powder, baking powder and salt into a large bowl. Stir in the brown sugar and the crushed chocolate balls.

Lightly beat the eggs in a large bowl then beat in the buttermilk and butter. Make a well in the centre of the dry ingredients and pour in the beaten liquid ingredients. Stir gently until just combined; do not over-mix.

Spoon the mixture into the prepared muffin tin. Bake in the preheated oven for about 20 minutes until well risen and firm to the touch.

Leave the muffins in the tin for 5 minutes then transfer to a wire rack and leave to cool.

To make the icing, melt the chocolate in a heatproof bowl set over a pan of gently simmering water. Remove from the heat. Put the butter in a large bowl and beat until fluffy. Sift in the icing sugar and beat together until smooth and creamy. Add the melted chocolate and beat together until well mixed.

Spread the icing on top of the muffins and decorate each with one of the reserved chocolate balls.

Double Chocolate Muffins

makes 12

oil or melted butter,
for greasing (if using)

100 g/3½ oz butter,
softened

125 g/4½ oz caster sugar

100 g/3½ oz dark
muscovado sugar

2 eggs

150 ml/5 fl oz soured cream

5 tbsp milk

250 g/9 oz plain flour

1 tsp bicarbonate of soda

2 tbsp cocoa powder

190 g/6½ oz plain
chocolate chips

Preheat the oven to 190°C/375°F/Gas Mark 5. Grease a 12-cup muffin tin or line with 12 paper cases. Place the butter and both sugars in a large bowl and beat well. Beat in the eggs, soured cream and milk until well mixed.

Sift together the flour, bicarbonate of soda and cocoa powder into a large bowl. Make a well in the centre of the dry ingredients and pour in the beaten liquid ingredients. Add the chocolate chips and stir gently until just combined; do not over-mix.

Spoon the mixture into the prepared muffin tin. Bake in the preheated oven for 25–30 minutes until well risen and firm to the touch.

Leave the muffins in the tin for 5 minutes then serve warm or transfer to a wire rack and leave to cool.

Chocolate Cream Muffins

makes 12

oil or melted butter, for greasing (if using)

225 g/8 oz plain flour

55 g/2 oz cocoa powder

1 tbsp baking powder

pinch of salt

115 g/4 oz soft light brown sugar

150 g/5½ oz white chocolate chips

2 eggs

250 ml/9 fl oz double cream

85 g/3 oz butter, melted and cooled

Preheat the oven to 200°C/400°F/Gas Mark 6. Grease a 12-cup muffin tin or line with 12 paper cases. Sift together the flour, cocoa powder, baking powder and salt into a large bowl. Stir in the sugar and chocolate chips.

Lightly beat the eggs in a large bowl then beat in the cream and butter. Make a well in the centre of the dry ingredients and pour in the beaten liquid ingredients. Stir gently until just combined; do not over-mix.

Spoon the mixture into the prepared muffin tin. Bake in the preheated oven for about 20 minutes until well risen and firm to the touch.

Leave the muffins in the tin for 5 minutes then serve warm or transfer to a wire rack and leave to cool.

Chocolate Orange Muffins

makes 10

oil or melted butter,
for greasing (if using)

125 g/4½ oz self-raising
flour

125 g/4½ oz self-raising
wholemeal flour

25 g/1 oz ground almonds

55 g/2 oz soft brown sugar

rind and juice of 1 orange

175 g/6 oz cream cheese

2 eggs

55 g/2 oz plain
chocolate chips

Preheat the oven to 190°C/375°F/Gas Mark 5. Grease 10 cups of a 12-cup muffin tin or line with 10 paper cases.

Sift together both flours into a large bowl and add the ground almonds and sugar.

In a large bowl, beat together the orange rind and juice, cream cheese and eggs. Make a well in the centre of the dry ingredients and pour in the beaten liquid ingredients. Add the chocolate chips. Stir gently until just combined; do not over-mix.

Spoon the mixture into the prepared muffin tin. Bake in the preheated oven for 25–30 minutes until well risen, golden brown and firm to the touch.

Leave the muffins in the tin for 5 minutes then serve warm or transfer to a wire rack and leave to cool.

Mint Chocolate Chip Muffins

makes 12

oil or melted butter, for greasing (if using)

280 g/10 oz plain flour

1 tbsp baking powder

pinch of salt

115 g/4 oz caster sugar

150 g/5½ oz plain chocolate chips

2 eggs

250 ml/9 fl oz milk

85 g/3 oz butter, melted and cooled

1 tsp peppermint extract

1–2 drops of green food colouring (optional)

icing sugar, for dusting

Preheat the oven to 200°C/400°F/Gas Mark 6. Grease a 12-cup muffin tin or line with 12 paper cases. Sift together the flour, baking powder and salt into a large bowl. Stir in the caster sugar and chocolate chips.

Lightly beat the eggs in a large bowl then beat in the milk, butter and peppermint extract. Add the food colouring, if using, to colour the mixture a very subtle shade of green. Make a well in the centre of the dry ingredients and pour in the beaten liquid ingredients. Stir gently until just combined; do not over-mix.

Spoon the mixture into the prepared muffin tin. Bake in the preheated oven for about 20 minutes until well risen and firm to the touch.

Leave the muffins in the tin for 5 minutes then serve warm or transfer to a wire rack and leave to cool. Dust with icing sugar before serving.

Spiced Chocolate Muffins

makes 12

oil or melted butter, for greasing (if using)

100 g/3½ oz butter, softened

150 g/5½ oz caster sugar

115 g/4 oz soft light brown sugar

2 large eggs

150 ml/5 fl oz soured cream

5 tbsp milk

250 g/9 oz plain flour

1 tsp bicarbonate of soda

2 tbsp cocoa powder

1 tsp allspice

200 g/7 oz plain chocolate chips

Preheat the oven to 190°C/375°F/Gas Mark 5. Grease a 12-cup muffin tin or line with 12 paper cases. Place the butter and both sugars in a large bowl and beat together, then beat in the eggs, soured cream and milk until thoroughly mixed.

Sift together the flour, bicarbonate of soda, cocoa powder and allspice into a large bowl. Make a well in the centre of the dry ingredients and pour in the beaten liquid ingredients. Add the chocolate chips. Stir gently until just combined; do not over-mix.

Spoon the mixture into the prepared muffin tin. Bake in the preheated oven for 25–30 minutes until well risen and firm to the touch.

Leave the muffins in the tin for 5 minutes then serve warm or transfer to a wire rack and leave to cool.

Decadent Chocolate Dessert Muffins

makes 12

oil or melted butter,
for greasing

225 g/8 oz plain flour

55 g/2 oz cocoa powder

1 tbsp baking powder

pinch of salt

115 g/4 oz soft light brown
sugar

2 eggs

250 ml/9 fl oz single cream

85 g/3 oz butter, melted
and cooled

85 g/3 oz plain chocolate

chocolate sauce

200 g/7 oz plain chocolate

25 g/1 oz butter

50 ml/2 fl oz single cream

Preheat the oven to 200°C/400°F/Gas Mark 6. Grease a 12-cup muffin tin or line with 12 paper cases. Sift together the flour, cocoa powder, baking powder and salt into a large bowl. Stir in the sugar.

Lightly beat the eggs in a large bowl then beat in the cream and butter. Make a well in the centre of the dry ingredients and pour in the beaten liquid ingredients. Stir gently until just combined; do not over-mix.

Break the chocolate evenly into 12 pieces. Spoon half of the mixture into the prepared muffin tin. Place a piece of chocolate in the centre of each then spoon in the remaining mixture. Bake in the preheated oven for about 20 minutes until well risen and firm to the touch.

Meanwhile, make the sauce. Melt the chocolate and butter together in a heatproof bowl set over a pan of gently simmering water. Stir until blended then stir in the cream and mix together. Remove from the heat and stir until smooth.

Leave the muffins in the tin for 5 minutes, then remove from the tin and place on serving plates. Serve warm with the sauce.

Triple Chocolate Muffins

makes 12

oil or melted butter,
for greasing (if using)

250 g/9 oz plain flour

25 g/1 oz cocoa powder

2 tsp baking powder

½ tsp bicarbonate of soda

100 g/3½ oz plain
chocolate chips

100 g/3½ oz white
chocolate chips

85 g/3 oz light
muscovado sugar

2 eggs, lightly beaten

300 ml/10 fl oz
soured cream

85 g/3 oz butter, melted

Preheat the oven to 200°C/400°F/Gas Mark 6. Grease a 12-cup muffin tin or line with 12 paper cases. Sift together the flour, cocoa powder, baking powder and bicarbonate of soda into a large bowl, then stir in the plain and white chocolate chips. Stir in the sugar.

Lightly beat the eggs in a large bowl with the soured cream and butter. Make a well in the centre of the dry ingredients and pour in the beaten liquid ingredients. Stir gently until just combined; do not over-mix.

Spoon the mixture into the prepared muffin tin. Bake in the preheated oven for 20 minutes until well risen and firm to the touch.

Leave the muffins in the tin for 5 minutes then serve warm or transfer to a wire rack and leave to cool.

Dark Chocolate & Ginger Muffins

makes 12

oil or melted butter, for greasing (if using)

225 g/8 oz plain flour

55 g/2 oz cocoa powder

1 tbsp baking powder

1 tbsp ground ginger

pinch of salt

115 g/4 oz soft dark brown sugar

3 pieces preserved ginger in syrup, finely chopped, plus 2 tbsp syrup from the jar

2 eggs

220 ml/7½ fl oz milk

85 g/3 oz butter, melted and cooled

Preheat the oven to 200°C/400°F/Gas Mark 6. Grease a 12-cup muffin tin or line with 12 paper cases. Sift together the flour, cocoa powder, baking powder, ground ginger and salt into a large bowl. Stir in the sugar and preserved ginger.

Lightly beat the eggs in a large bowl then beat in the milk, butter and ginger syrup. Make a well in the centre of the dry ingredients and pour in the beaten liquid ingredients. Stir gently until just combined; do not over-mix.

Spoon the mixture into the prepared muffin tin. Bake in the preheated oven for about 20 minutes until well risen and firm to the touch.

Leave the muffins in the tin for 5 minutes then serve warm or transfer to a wire rack and leave to cool.

Chocolate Cinnamon Muffins

makes 12

oil or melted butter,
for greasing (if using)

225 g/8 oz plain flour

55 g/2 oz cocoa powder

1 tbsp baking powder

½ tsp ground cinnamon

pinch of salt

115 g/4 oz soft light brown
sugar

150 g/5½ oz plain
chocolate chips

2 eggs

250 ml/9 fl oz milk

85 g/3 oz butter, melted
and cooled

Preheat the oven to 200°C/400°F/Gas Mark 6. Grease a 12-cup muffin tin or line with 12 paper cases. Sift together the flour, cocoa powder, baking powder, cinnamon and salt into a large bowl. Stir in the sugar and chocolate chips.

Lightly beat the eggs in a large bowl then beat in the milk and butter. Make a well in the centre of the dry ingredients and pour in the beaten liquid ingredients. Stir gently until just combined; do not over-mix.

Spoon the mixture into the prepared muffin tin. Bake in the preheated oven for about 20 minutes until well risen and firm to the touch.

Leave the muffins in the tin for 5 minutes then serve warm or transfer to a wire rack and leave to cool.

Marbled Chocolate Muffins

makes 12

oil or melted butter,
for greasing (if using)

280 g/10 oz plain flour

1 tbsp baking powder

pinch of salt

115 g/4 oz caster sugar

2 eggs

250 ml/9 fl oz milk

85 g/3 oz butter, melted
and cooled

1 tsp vanilla extract

2 tbsp cocoa powder

Preheat the oven to 200°C/400°F/Gas Mark 6. Grease a 12-cup muffin tin or line with 12 paper cases. Sift together the flour, baking powder and salt into a large bowl. Stir in the sugar.

Lightly beat the eggs in a large bowl then beat in the milk, butter and vanilla extract. Make a well in the centre of the dry ingredients and pour in the beaten liquid ingredients. Gently stir until just combined; do not over-mix.

Divide the mixture between 2 bowls. Sift the cocoa powder into one bowl and stir into the mixture. Using teaspoons, spoon the mixtures into the prepared muffin tin alternating the chocolate mixture and the plain mixture.

Bake in the preheated oven for about 20 minutes until well risen, golden brown and firm to the touch.

Leave the muffins in the tin for 5 minutes then serve warm or transfer to a wire rack and leave to cool.

Rocky Road Chocolate Muffins

makes 12

oil or melted butter,
for greasing (if using)

225 g/8 oz plain flour

55 g/2 oz cocoa powder

1 tbsp baking powder

pinch of salt

115 g/4 oz caster sugar

100 g/3½ oz white
chocolate chips

50 g/1¾ oz white
mini marshmallows,
cut in half

2 eggs

250 ml/9 fl oz milk

85 g/3 oz butter, melted
and cooled

Preheat the oven to 200°C/400°F/Gas Mark 6. Grease a 12-cup muffin tin or line with 12 paper cases. Sift together the flour, cocoa powder, baking powder and salt into a large bowl. Stir in the sugar, chocolate chips and marshmallows.

Lightly beat the eggs in a large bowl then beat in the milk and butter. Make a well in the centre of the dry ingredients and pour in the beaten liquid ingredients. Gently stir until just combined; do not over-mix.

Spoon the mixture into the prepared muffin tin. Bake in the preheated oven for about 20 minutes until risen and firm to the touch.

Leave the muffins in the tin for 5 minutes then serve warm or transfer to a wire rack and leave to cool.

Marshmallow Muffins

makes 12

oil or melted butter,
for greasing (if using)

280 g/10 oz plain flour

6 tbsp cocoa powder

3 tsp baking powder

85 g/3 oz caster sugar

1 egg, beaten

300 ml/10 fl oz milk

70 g/2½ oz butter, melted

100 g/3½ oz milk
chocolate chips

55 g/2 oz white mini
marshmallows

Preheat the oven to 190°C/375°F/Gas Mark 5. Grease a 12-cup muffin tin or line with 12 paper cases.

Sift together the flour, cocoa powder and baking powder into a large bowl. Stir in the sugar.

Beat together the egg, milk and butter in a large bowl until blended. Make a well in the centre of the dry ingredients and pour in the beaten liquid ingredients. Lightly stir in the chocolate chips and marshmallows. Stir gently until just combined; do not over-mix.

Spoon the mixture into the prepared muffin tin. Bake in the preheated oven for 20–25 minutes until well risen and firm to the touch.

Leave the muffins in the tin for 5 minutes then serve warm or transfer to a wire rack and leave to cool.

Sugar-free Chocolate Muffins

makes 12

oil or melted butter, for greasing (if using)

225 g/8 oz plain flour

1 tbsp baking powder

1 tbsp cocoa powder

½ tsp mixed spice

2 eggs

4 tbsp vegetable oil

175 ml/6 fl oz unsweetened orange juice

rind of ½ orange

100 g/3½ oz fresh blueberries

Preheat the oven to 200°C/400°F/Gas Mark 6. Grease a 12-cup muffin tin or line with 12 paper cases. Sift together the flour, baking powder, cocoa powder and mixed spice into a large bowl.

Lightly beat the eggs with the oil in a large bowl. Pour in the orange juice, then add the rind and the blueberries and gently stir together to mix. Make a well in the centre of the dry ingredients and pour in the beaten liquid ingredients. Gently stir until just combined; do not over-mix.

Spoon the mixture into the prepared muffin tin. Bake in the preheated oven for 20 minutes until well risen and firm to the touch.

Leave the muffins in the tin for 5 minutes then serve warm or transfer to a wire rack and leave to cool.

3

Something
Special

Birthday Muffins

makes 12

oil or melted butter,
for greasing (if using)

280 g/10 oz plain flour

1 tbsp baking powder

pinch of salt

115 g/4 oz caster sugar

2 eggs

250 ml/9 fl oz milk

85 g/3 oz butter, melted
and cooled

finely grated rind of
1 lemon

12 candles and
candleholders,
to decorate

icing

85 g/3 oz butter, softened

175 g/6 oz icing sugar

Preheat the oven to 200°C/400°F/Gas Mark 6. Grease a 12-cup muffin tin or line with 12 paper cases. Sift together the flour, baking powder and salt into a large bowl. Stir in the caster sugar.

Lightly beat the eggs in a large bowl then beat in the milk, butter and lemon rind. Make a well in the centre of the dry ingredients and pour in the beaten liquid ingredients. Stir gently until just combined; do not over-mix.

Spoon the mixture into the prepared muffin tin. Bake in the preheated oven for about 20 minutes until well risen, golden brown and firm to the touch.

Leave the muffins in the tin for 5 minutes then transfer to a wire rack and leave to cool.

To make the icing, put the butter in a large bowl and beat until fluffy. Sift in the icing sugar and beat together until smooth and creamy.

When the muffins are cold, spread each one with a little of the icing then place a candleholder and candle on top.

Anniversary Muffins

makes 12

oil or melted butter,
for greasing (if using)

280 g/10 oz plain flour

1 tbsp baking powder

pinch of salt

115 g/4 oz caster sugar

2 eggs

250 ml/9 fl oz buttermilk

85 g/3 oz butter, melted
and cooled

finely grated rind of
1 lemon

silver or gold dragées,
to decorate

icing

85 g/3 oz butter, softened

175 g/6 oz icing sugar

Preheat the oven to 200°C/400°F/Gas Mark 6. Grease a 12-cup muffin tin or line with 12 paper cases. Sift together the flour, baking powder and salt into a large bowl. Stir in the caster sugar.

Lightly beat the eggs in a large bowl then beat in the buttermilk, butter and lemon rind. Make a well in the centre of the dry ingredients and pour in the beaten liquid ingredients. Stir gently until just combined; do not over-mix.

Spoon the mixture into the prepared muffin tin. Bake in the preheated oven for about 20 minutes until well risen, golden brown and firm to the touch.

Leave the muffins in the tin for 5 minutes then transfer to a wire rack and leave to cool.

To make the icing, put the butter in a large bowl and beat until fluffy. Sift in the icing sugar and beat together until smooth and creamy.

When the muffins are cold, put the icing in a piping bag fitted with a large star nozzle and pipe circles on top of each muffin to cover the top. Sprinkle with the silver dragées to decorate.

Valentine Heart Muffins

makes 12

oil or melted butter,
for greasing

225 g/8 oz plain flour

55 g/2 oz cocoa powder

1 tbsp baking powder

pinch of salt

115 g/4 oz soft light brown
sugar

2 eggs

250 ml/9 fl oz buttermilk

85 g/3 oz butter, melted
and cooled

marzipan hearts

icing sugar, for dusting

70 g/2½ oz marzipan,
coloured with a few
drops of red food
colouring

icing

55 g/2 oz plain chocolate

115 g/4 oz butter, softened

225 g/8 oz icing sugar

To make the marzipan hearts, dust a work surface with icing sugar then roll out the marzipan to a thickness of 5 mm/¼ inch. Using a small heart-shaped cutter, cut out 12 hearts. Line a tray with greaseproof paper, dust with icing sugar and place the hearts on it. Leave for 3–4 hours until dry.

Preheat the oven to 200°C/400°F/Gas Mark 6. Grease a 12-cup heart-shaped muffin tin. Sift together the flour, cocoa powder, baking powder and salt into a large bowl. Stir in the brown sugar.

Lightly beat the eggs in a large bowl then beat in the buttermilk and butter. Make a well in the centre of the dry ingredients and pour in the beaten liquid ingredients. Stir gently until just combined; do not over-mix.

Spoon the mixture into the prepared muffin tin. Bake in the preheated oven for about 20 minutes until well risen and firm to the touch.

Leave the muffins in the tin for 5 minutes then transfer to a wire rack and leave to cool.

To make the icing, melt the chocolate in a heatproof bowl set over a pan of gently simmering water. Remove from the heat. Put the butter in a large bowl and beat until fluffy. Sift in the icing sugar and beat together until smooth and creamy. Add the melted chocolate and beat together. Spread the icing on top of the muffins then decorate each with a marzipan heart.

Christmas Muffins

makes 18

oil or melted butter, for greasing (if using)

225 g/8 oz plain flour

2 tsp baking powder

½ tsp salt

55 g/2 oz caster sugar

4 tbsp butter, melted

2 large eggs, lightly beaten

175 ml/6 fl oz milk

115 g/4 oz fresh cranberries

25 g/1 oz freshly grated Parmesan cheese

Preheat the oven to 200°C/400°F/Gas Mark 6. Grease a 12-cup muffin tin and a 6-cup muffin tin or line with 18 paper cases. Sift the flour, baking powder and salt into a large bowl. Stir in the caster sugar.

Combine the butter, beaten eggs and milk in a large bowl. Make a well in the centre of the dry ingredients and pour in the beaten liquid ingredients. Add the cranberries and stir gently until just combined; do not over-mix.

Spoon the mixture into the prepared muffin tins. Sprinkle the grated Parmesan cheese over the top. Bake in the preheated oven for 20 minutes until well risen, golden brown and firm to the touch.

Leave the muffins in the tin for 5 minutes then serve warm or transfer to a wire rack and leave to cool.

Easter Muffins

makes 12

oil or melted butter,
for greasing (if using)

225 g/8 oz plain flour

55 g/2 oz cocoa powder

1 tbsp baking powder

pinch of salt

115 g/4 oz soft light brown
sugar

2 eggs

250 ml/9 fl oz buttermilk

85 g/3 oz butter, melted
and cooled

250 g/9 oz sugar-coated
mini chocolate eggs,
to decorate

icing

85 g/3 oz butter, softened

175 g/6 oz icing sugar

1 tbsp milk

Preheat the oven to 200°C/400°F/Gas Mark 6. Grease a 12-cup muffin tin or line with 12 paper cases. Sift together the flour, cocoa powder, baking powder and salt into a large bowl. Stir in the brown sugar.

Lightly beat the eggs in a large bowl then beat in the buttermilk and butter. Make a well in the centre of the dry ingredients and pour in the beaten liquid ingredients. Stir gently until just combined; do not over-mix.

Spoon the mixture into the prepared muffin tin. Bake in the preheated oven for about 20 minutes until well risen and firm to the touch.

Leave the muffins in the tin for 5 minutes then transfer to a wire rack and leave to cool.

To make the icing, put the butter in a large bowl and beat until fluffy. Sift in the icing sugar and beat together until smooth and creamy, then beat in the milk.

When the muffins are cold, put the icing in a piping bag fitted with a large star nozzle and pipe a circle around the top of each muffin to form a 'nest'. Place chocolate eggs in the centre of each nest to decorate.

Rose-topped Wedding Muffins

makes 12

oil or melted butter,
for greasing (if using)

280 g/10 oz plain flour

1 tbsp baking powder

pinch of salt

115 g/4 oz caster sugar

2 eggs

250 ml/9 fl oz milk

85 g/3 oz butter, melted
and cooled

1 tsp vanilla extract

12 ready-made sugar roses
or fresh rose petals or
buds, to decorate

icing

175 g/6 oz icing sugar

3–4 tsp hot water

Preheat the oven to 200°C/400°F/Gas Mark 6. Increase the quantity of ingredients according to the number of wedding guests invited, working in double quantities to make 24 muffins each time. Grease the appropriate number of muffin tins or line with paper cases. Sift together the flour, baking powder and salt into a large bowl. Stir in the caster sugar.

Lightly beat the eggs in a large bowl then beat in the milk, butter and vanilla extract. Make a well in the centre of the dry ingredients and pour in the beaten liquid ingredients. Stir gently until just combined; do not over-mix.

Spoon the mixture into the prepared muffin tin or tins. Bake in the preheated oven for about 20 minutes until well risen, golden brown and firm to the touch.

Leave the muffins in the tin or tins for 5 minutes then transfer to a wire rack and leave to cool. Store the muffins in the freezer until required.

On the day of serving, if using fresh flowers, rinse and leave to dry on kitchen paper. For the icing, sift the icing sugar into a bowl. Add the water and stir until the mixture is smooth and thick enough to coat the back of a wooden spoon. Spoon the icing on top of each muffin then top with sugar roses.

Mother's Day Breakfast Muffins

makes 12

oil or melted butter,
for greasing (if using)

280 g/10 oz plain flour

1 tbsp baking powder

pinch of salt

115 g/4 oz caster sugar

2 eggs

250 ml/9 fl oz milk

85 g/3 oz butter, melted
and cooled

1 tsp orange extract

fresh strawberries and
fruit juice, to serve

icing sugar, for dusting

Preheat the oven to 200°C/400°F/Gas Mark 6. Grease a 12-cup muffin tin or line with 12 paper cases. Sift together the flour, baking powder and salt into a large bowl. Stir in the caster sugar.

Lightly beat the eggs in a large bowl then beat in the milk, butter and orange extract. Make a well in the centre of the dry ingredients and pour in the beaten liquid ingredients. Stir gently until just combined; do not over-mix.

Spoon the mixture into the prepared muffin tin. Bake in the preheated oven for about 20 minutes until well risen, golden brown and firm to the touch.

Leave the muffins in the tin for 5 minutes. Meanwhile, arrange the strawberries in a bowl and pour the juice into a glass.

Dust the muffins with icing sugar. Serve warm with the strawberries and juice.

Fresh Flower Muffins

makes 12

oil or melted butter, for greasing (if using)

280 g/10 oz plain flour

1 tbsp baking powder

pinch of salt

115 g/4 oz caster sugar

2 eggs

250 ml/9 fl oz buttermilk

85 g/3 oz butter, melted and cooled

finely grated rind of 1 lemon

12 edible flower heads, such as lavender, nasturtiums, violets, primroses or roses, to decorate

icing

85 g/3 oz butter, softened

175 g/6 oz icing sugar

Preheat the oven to 200°C/400°F/Gas Mark 6. Grease a 12-cup muffin tin or line with 12 paper cases. Carefully wash the flower heads and leave to dry on kitchen paper.

Sift together the flour, baking powder and salt into a large bowl. Stir in the caster sugar.

Lightly beat the eggs in a large bowl then beat in the buttermilk, butter and lemon rind. Make a well in the centre of the dry ingredients and pour in the beaten liquid ingredients. Stir gently until just combined; do not over-mix.

Spoon the mixture into the prepared muffin tin. Bake in the preheated oven for about 20 minutes until well risen, golden brown and firm to the touch.

Leave the muffins in the tin for 5 minutes then transfer to a wire rack and leave to cool.

To make the icing, put the butter in a large bowl and beat until fluffy. Sift in the icing sugar and beat together until smooth and creamy. When the muffins are cold, put the icing in a piping bag fitted with a large star nozzle and pipe circles on top of each muffin to cover the top. Just before serving, place a flower head on top to decorate.

Spiced Wholemeal Muffins

makes 6

oil or melted butter,
for greasing (if using)

125 g/4½ oz plain flour

½ tsp baking powder

55 g/2 oz wholemeal flour

½ tsp allspice

1 tbsp vegetable oil

1 egg

150 ml/5 fl oz buttermilk

1 tbsp freshly squeezed
orange juice

1 tsp marmalade,
for glazing

filling

100 g/3½ oz thick natural
yogurt

1 tsp marmalade

½ tsp grated orange zest

100 g/3½ oz fresh
raspberries

Preheat the oven to 160°C/325°F/Gas Mark 3. Grease a 6-cup muffin tin or line with 6 paper cases. Sift together the plain flour and baking powder into a large bowl. Using a fork, stir in the wholemeal flour and allspice until thoroughly mixed. Pour in the oil and rub into the flour mixture with your fingertips.

Lightly beat the egg in a large bowl, then beat in the buttermilk and orange juice. Make a well in the centre of the dry ingredients and pour in the beaten liquid ingredients. Stir gently until just combined; do not over-mix.

Spoon the mixture into the prepared muffin tin. Bake in the preheated oven for 20 minutes until well risen, golden brown and firm to the touch.

Leave the muffins in the tin for 5 minutes then transfer to a wire rack. Brush with marmalade and cool.

For the filling, mix the yogurt with the marmalade and orange zest. Cut the warm muffins in half and fill with the yogurt mixture and raspberries.

Baby Shower Muffins

makes 12

oil or melted butter,
for greasing (if using)

280 g/10 oz plain flour

1 tbsp baking powder

pinch of salt

115 g/4 oz caster sugar

2 eggs

250 ml/9 fl oz buttermilk

85 g/3 oz butter, melted
and cooled

finely grated rind of
1 lemon

12 pink or blue sugared
almonds, to decorate

icing

175 g/6 oz icing sugar

3–4 tsp hot water

1–2 drops of red or blue
food colouring

Preheat the oven to 200°C/400°F/Gas Mark 6. Grease a 12-cup muffin tin or line with 12 paper cases. Sift together the flour, baking powder and salt into a large bowl. Stir in the caster sugar.

Lightly beat the eggs in a large bowl then beat in the buttermilk, butter and lemon rind. Make a well in the centre of the dry ingredients and pour in the beaten liquid ingredients. Stir gently until just combined; do not over-mix.

Spoon the mixture into the prepared muffin tin. Bake in the preheated oven for about 20 minutes until well risen, golden brown and firm to the touch.

Leave the muffins in the tin for 5 minutes then transfer to a wire rack and leave to cool.

When the muffins are cold, make the icing. Sift the icing sugar into a bowl. Add the water and stir until the mixture is smooth and thick enough to coat the back of a wooden spoon. Add 1–2 drops of food colouring and stir into the icing until evenly coloured pink or pale blue.

Spoon the icing on top of each muffin. Top with a sugared almond and leave to set for about 30 minutes before serving.

Gluten- and Dairy-free Banana Muffins

makes 12

150 g/5½ oz gluten-free plain flour

1 tsp gluten-free baking powder

pinch of salt

150 g/5½ oz caster sugar

6 tbsp dairy-free milk

2 eggs, lightly beaten

150 g/5½ oz dairy-free margarine, melted

2 small bananas, mashed

icing

50 g/1¾ oz vegan cream cheese

2 tbsp dairy-free margarine

¼ tsp ground cinnamon

90 g/3¼ oz icing sugar

Preheat the oven to 200°C/400°F/Gas Mark 6. Grease a 12-cup muffin tin or line with 12 paper cases. Sift together the flour, baking powder and salt into a large bowl. Stir in the sugar.

Combine the milk, eggs and margarine together in a large bowl. Make a well in the centre of the dry ingredients and pour in the liquid ingredients. Add the bananas. Stir gently until just combined; do not over-mix.

Spoon the mixture into the prepared muffin tin. Bake in the preheated oven for 20 minutes until well risen, golden brown and firm to the touch.

Leave the muffins in the tin for 5 minutes then transfer to a wire rack and leave to cool.

To make the icing, beat the cream cheese and margarine together in a bowl, then beat in the cinnamon and icing sugar until smooth and creamy. Chill the frosting in the refrigerator for about 15 minutes to firm up, then top each muffin with a spoonful.

Cherry & Coconut Muffins

makes 12

oil or melted butter,
for greasing (if using)

125 g/4½ oz glacé cherries

280 g/10 oz plain flour

1 tbsp baking powder

pinch of salt

115 g/4 oz caster sugar

40 g/1½ oz desiccated
coconut

2 eggs

250 ml/9 fl oz coconut milk

85 g/3 oz butter, melted
and cooled

1 tsp vanilla extract

12 whole fresh cherries
on their stalks

Preheat the oven to 200°C/400°F/Gas Mark 6. Grease a 12-cup muffin tin or line with 12 paper cases. Cut the glacé cherries into small pieces.

Sift together the flour, baking powder and salt into a large bowl. Stir in the sugar, desiccated coconut and chopped glacé cherries.

Lightly beat the eggs in a large bowl then beat in the coconut milk, butter and vanilla extract. Make a well in the centre of the dry ingredients and pour in the beaten liquid ingredients. Stir gently until just combined; do not over-mix.

Spoon the mixture into the prepared muffin tin. Top each muffin with a whole fresh cherry. Bake in the preheated oven for about 20 minutes until well risen, golden brown and firm to the touch.

Leave the muffins in the tin for 5 minutes then serve warm or transfer to a wire rack and leave to cool.

Marzipan Muffins

makes 12

oil or melted butter, for greasing (if using)

175 g/6 oz marzipan

280 g/10 oz plain flour

1 tbsp baking powder

pinch of salt

115 g/4 oz caster sugar

2 eggs

200 ml/7 fl oz milk

85 g/3 oz butter, melted and cooled

1 tsp almond essence

12 whole blanched almonds

Preheat the oven to 200°C/400°F/Gas Mark 6. Grease a 12-cup muffin tin or line with 12 paper cases.

Cut the marzipan into 12 equal pieces. Roll each piece into a ball, and then flatten with the palm of your hand, making sure that they are no larger than the paper cases.

Sift together the flour, baking powder and salt into a large bowl. Stir in the sugar. Lightly beat the eggs in a large bowl then beat in the milk, butter and almond essence.

Make a well in the centre of the dry ingredients and pour in the beaten liquid ingredients. Stir gently until just combined; do not over-mix. Spoon half of the mixture into the paper cases.

Place a piece of marzipan in the centre of each, then spoon in the remaining mixture. Top each muffin with a whole blanched almond. Bake in the preheated oven for 20 minutes until well risen, golden brown and firm to the touch.

Leave in the tin for 5 minutes then serve warm or transfer to a wire rack to cool.

Mini Muffins with Sticky Toffee Sauce

makes 20

oil or melted butter, for greasing (if using)

200 g/7 oz stoned dried dates, chopped

200 ml/7 fl oz water

1 tsp bicarbonate of soda

55 g/2 oz butter

175 g/6 oz self-raising flour

150 g/5½ oz caster sugar

1 tsp vanilla extract

2 eggs, beaten

toffee sauce

150 ml/5 fl oz double cream

1 tbsp golden syrup

70 g/2½ oz soft light brown sugar

55 g/2 oz butter

Preheat the oven to 180°C/350°F/Gas Mark 4. Grease 20 cups of two 12-cup mini muffin tins or line with 20 small paper cases.

Put the dates and water in a saucepan and bring to the boil. Cook over a low heat for 10 minutes, or until softened. Stir in the bicarbonate of soda and butter – it will froth up – and stir until the butter has melted.

Leave to cool slightly, then pour the mixture into a blender or food processor and process to a coarse purée.

Sift the flour into a large bowl and stir in the caster sugar. Add the vanilla extract, eggs and date purée and stir gently until just combined; do not over-mix.

Spoon the mixture into the prepared muffin tins. Bake in the preheated oven for 12–15 minutes until well risen.

To make the sauce, put all the ingredients in a small saucepan. Bring to the boil, stirring constantly, then reduce the heat and simmer for 10 minutes, or until thickened and glossy. Remove from the heat and leave to cool slightly.

Serve the muffins warm with the sauce poured over.

After Dinner Coffee Liqueur Muffins

makes 12

oil or melted butter, for greasing (if using)

2 tbsp instant coffee granules

2 tbsp boiling water

280 g/10 oz plain flour

1 tbsp baking powder

pinch of salt

115 g/4 oz soft light brown sugar

2 eggs

100 ml/3½ fl oz milk

85 g/3 oz butter, melted and cooled

6 tbsp coffee liqueur

40 g/1½ oz demerara sugar

Preheat the oven to 200°C/400°F/Gas Mark 6. Grease a 12-cup muffin tin or line with 12 paper cases. Put the coffee granules and boiling water in a cup and stir until dissolved. Leave to cool.

Meanwhile, sift together the flour, baking powder and salt into a large bowl. Stir in the brown sugar.

Lightly beat the eggs in a large bowl then beat in the milk, butter, dissolved coffee and liqueur. Make a well in the centre of the dry ingredients and pour in the beaten liquid ingredients. Stir gently until just combined; do not over-mix.

Spoon the mixture into the prepared muffin tin. Sprinkle the demerara sugar over the tops of the muffins. Bake in the preheated oven for about 20 minutes until well risen, golden brown and firm to the touch.

Leave the muffins in the tin for 5 minutes then serve or transfer to a wire rack and leave to cool.

Irish Coffee Muffins

makes 12

oil or melted butter,
for greasing (if using)

280 g/10 oz plain flour

1 tbsp baking powder

pinch of salt

85 g/3 oz butter

55 g/2 oz sugar

1 large egg, beaten

125 ml/4 fl oz double cream

1 tsp almond essence

2 tbsp strong coffee

2 tbsp coffee-flavoured
liqueur

4 tbsp Irish whiskey

whipped cream and icing
sugar, to serve (optional)

Preheat the oven to 200°C/400°F/Gas Mark 6. Grease
a 12-cup muffin tin or line with 12 paper cases. Sift together
the flour, baking powder and salt into a large bowl.

In a separate large bowl, cream the butter and sugar together,
then stir in the egg. Pour in the cream, almond essence, coffee,
liqueur and whiskey and stir together. Make a well in the centre
of the dry ingredients and pour in the liquid ingredients. Stir
gently until just combined; do not over-mix.

Spoon the mixture into the prepared muffin tin. Bake in the
preheated oven for 20 minutes until well risen, golden brown
and firm to the touch.

Leave the muffins in the tin for 5 minutes then transfer to
a wire rack and leave to cool. If liked, cut the tops off the
muffins, fill with whipped double cream and sprinkle with icing
sugar to serve.

Brandied Cherry Muffins

makes 12

oil or melted butter,
for greasing (if using)

225 g/8 oz plain flour

1 tbsp baking powder

pinch of salt

3 tbsp butter

2 tbsp caster sugar

1 egg, beaten

200 ml/7 fl oz milk

2 tsp cherry brandy

300 g/10½ oz drained
canned cherries,
chopped

Preheat the oven to 200°C/400°F/Gas Mark 6. Grease a 12-cup muffin tin or line with 12 paper cases.

Sift together the flour, baking powder and salt into a large bowl.

In a large bowl, cream together the butter and sugar, then stir in the egg. Pour in the milk and cherry brandy, then add the cherries and gently stir together. Make a well in the centre of the dry ingredients and pour in the liquid ingredients. Stir gently until just combined; do not over-mix.

Spoon the mixture into the prepared muffin tin. Bake in the preheated oven for 20–25 minutes until well risen, golden brown and firm to the touch.

Leave the muffins in the tin for 5 minutes then serve warm or transfer to a wire rack and leave to cool.

Low-fat Banana & Date Muffins

makes 12

oil or melted butter,
for greasing (if using)

215 g/7½ oz plain flour

2 tsp baking powder

¼ tsp salt

½ tsp mixed spice

5 tbsp caster sugar

2 egg whites

2 ripe bananas, sliced

75 g/2¾ oz ready-to-eat
dried dates, stoned and
chopped

4 tbsp skimmed milk

5 tbsp maple syrup

Preheat the oven to 200°C/400°F/Gas Mark 6. Grease a 12-cup muffin tin or line with 12 paper cases.

Sift together the flour, baking powder, salt and mixed spice into a large bowl. Add the sugar and mix together.

In a separate large bowl, whisk together the egg whites. Mash the sliced bananas in another bowl, then add them to the egg whites. Add the dates, then pour in the milk and maple syrup and stir together gently to mix. Make a well in the centre of the dry ingredients and pour in the liquid ingredients. Stir gently until just combined; do not over-mix.

Spoon the mixture into the prepared muffin tin. Bake in the preheated oven for 20–25 minutes until well risen, golden brown and firm to the touch.

Leave the muffins in the tin for 5 minutes then serve warm or transfer to a wire rack and leave to cool.

Savoury

Sour Cream Muffins with Chives

makes 12

oil or melted butter, for greasing (if using)

280 g/10 oz plain flour

2 tsp baking powder

½ tsp bicarbonate of soda

25 g/1 oz Cheddar cheese, grated

35 g/1¼ oz fresh chives, finely snipped, plus extra to garnish

1 egg, lightly beaten

200 ml/7 fl oz soured cream

100 ml/3½ fl oz natural yogurt

55 g/2 oz butter, melted and cooled

Preheat the oven to 200°C/400°F/Gas Mark 6. Grease a 12-cup muffin tin or line with 12 paper cases.

Sift the flour, baking powder and bicarbonate of soda into a large bowl. Add the cheese and chives and mix together well.

In a large bowl, lightly mix together the egg, cream, yogurt and butter. Make a well in the centre of the dry ingredients and pour in the liquid ingredients. Stir gently until just combined; do not over-mix.

Spoon the mixture into the prepared muffin tin and sprinkle over the remaining chives. Bake in the preheated oven for 20 minutes until well risen, golden brown and firm to the touch.

Leave the muffins in the tin for 5 minutes then serve warm or transfer to a wire rack and leave to cool.

Polenta Muffins

makes 9

oil or melted butter,
for greasing (if using)

250 ml/9 fl oz milk

125 ml/4 fl oz vegetable oil

2 eggs, lightly beaten

2 tbsp butter, melted
and cooled

2 tbsp honey

1 tsp vanilla extract

175 g/6 oz plain flour

1 tbsp baking powder

115 g/4 oz polenta

50 g/1¾ oz sugar

½ tsp salt

Preheat the oven to 200°C/400°F/Gas Mark 6. Grease 9 cups of a 12-cup muffin tin or line with 9 paper cases.

In a bowl, combine the milk, oil, eggs, butter, honey and vanilla extract.

Sift the flour and baking powder into a large bowl and stir in the polenta, sugar and salt. Make a well in the centre of the dry ingredients and pour in the liquid ingredients. Stir gently until just combined; do not over-mix.

Spoon the mixture into the prepared muffin tin. Bake in the preheated oven for 15–20 minutes until well risen, golden brown and firm to the touch.

Leave the muffins in the tin for 5 minutes then serve warm or transfer to a wire rack and leave to cool.

Herb Muffins with Smoked Cheese

makes 12

oil or melted butter,
for greasing (if using)

280 g/10 oz plain flour

2 tsp baking powder

1/2 tsp bicarbonate of soda

25 g/1 oz smoked hard
cheese, such as
Applewood, grated

50 g/1¾ oz fresh parsley,
finely chopped

1 egg, lightly beaten

300 ml/10 fl oz thick
natural yogurt

55 g/2 oz butter,
melted and cooled

Preheat the oven to 200°C/400°F/Gas Mark 6. Grease a 12-cup muffin tin or line with 12 paper cases.

Sift the flour, baking powder and bicarbonate of soda into a large bowl. Add the cheese and the parsley and mix together well.

In a separate large bowl, lightly mix together the egg, yogurt and butter. Make a well in the centre of the dry ingredients and pour in the liquid ingredients. Stir gently until just combined; do not over-mix.

Spoon the mixture into the prepared muffin tin. Bake in the preheated oven for 20 minutes until well risen, golden brown and firm to the touch.

Leave the muffins in the tin for 5 minutes then serve warm or transfer to a wire rack and leave to cool.

Caramelized Onion Muffins

makes 12

oil or melted butter, for greasing (if using)

7 tbsp sunflower oil

3 onions, finely chopped

1 tbsp red wine vinegar

2 tsp sugar

280 g/10 oz plain flour

1 tbsp baking powder

pinch of salt

2 eggs

250 ml/9 fl oz buttermilk

pepper

Preheat the oven to 200°C/400°F/Gas Mark 6. Grease a 12-cup muffin tin or line with 12 paper cases.

Heat 2 tablespoons of the oil in a frying pan. Add the onions and cook, stirring for 3 minutes, until beginning to soften. Add the vinegar and sugar and cook, stirring occasionally, for a further 10 minutes, until golden brown. Remove from the heat and leave to cool.

Meanwhile, sift together the flour, baking powder, salt and pepper to taste into a large bowl.

Lightly beat the eggs in a large jug or bowl then beat in the buttermilk and remaining sunflower oil. Make a well in the centre of the dry ingredients, pour in the beaten liquid ingredients and add the onion mixture, reserving 4 tablespoons for the topping. Stir gently until just combined; do not over-mix.

Spoon the mixture into the prepared muffin tin. Sprinkle the reserved onion mixture on top of the muffins. Bake in the preheated oven for about 20 minutes until well risen, golden brown and firm to the touch.

Leave the muffins in the tin for 5 minutes then serve warm.

Potato & Pancetta Muffins

makes 12

oil or melted butter, for greasing (if using)

1 tbsp vegetable oil

3 shallots, finely chopped

350 g/12 oz self-raising flour

1 tsp salt

450 g/1 lb potatoes, cooked and mashed

2 eggs

350 ml/12 fl oz milk

125 ml/4 fl oz soured cream

1 tbsp finely snipped fresh chives

150 g/5½ oz pancetta, chopped

4 tbsp grated Red Leicester or Cheddar cheese

Preheat the oven to 200°C/400°F/Gas Mark 6. Grease a 12-cup muffin tin or line with 12 paper cases. Heat the oil in a frying pan, add the shallots and cook, stirring, for 2 minutes. Remove from the heat and leave to cool.

Meanwhile, sift together the flour and salt into a large bowl. In a separate large bowl, mix together the mashed potato, eggs, milk, soured cream, chives and half of the pancetta. Make a well in the centre of the dry ingredients and pour in the liquid ingredients. Stir gently until just combined; do not over-mix.

Spoon the mixture into the prepared muffin tin and sprinkle over the remaining pancetta, then sprinkle over the cheese. Bake in the preheated oven for 20 minutes until well risen, golden brown and firm to the touch.

Leave the muffins in the tin for 5 minutes then serve warm or transfer to a wire rack and leave to cool.

Spanish Manchego Muffins

makes 12

oil or melted butter,
for greasing (if using)

280 g/10 oz plain flour

1 tbsp baking powder

½ tsp salt

3 tbsp granulated sugar

2 eggs

175 ml/6 fl oz milk

150 ml/5 fl oz vegetable oil

400 g/14 oz courgettes,
grated

25 g/1 oz Manchego cheese,
grated

2 tbsp chopped fresh
flat-leaf parsley

Preheat the oven to 200°C/400°F/Gas Mark 6. Grease a 12-cup muffin tin or line with 12 paper cases.

Sift the flour, baking powder and salt into a large bowl. Add the sugar and mix together well.

In a separate large bowl, lightly beat the eggs. Stir in the milk and vegetable oil and mix together. Make a well in the centre of the dry ingredients and pour in the beaten liquid ingredients. Gently stir in the courgettes, cheese and parsley, until just combined; do not over-mix.

Spoon the mixture into the prepared muffin tin. Bake in the preheated oven for 25 minutes until well risen, golden brown and firm to the touch.

Leave the muffins in the tin for 5 minutes then serve warm or transfer to a wire rack and leave to cool.

Chilli Cornbread Muffins

makes 12

oil or melted butter, for greasing (if using)

175 g/6 oz plain flour

4 tsp baking powder

175 g/6 oz cornmeal or polenta

2 tbsp caster sugar

1 tsp salt

4 spring onions, trimmed and finely chopped

1 fresh red chilli, deseeded and finely chopped

3 eggs, beaten

150 ml/5 fl oz natural yogurt

150 ml/5 fl oz milk

Preheat the oven to 200°C/400°F/Gas Mark 6. Grease a 12-cup muffin tin or line with 12 paper cases.

Sift the flour and baking powder into a large bowl. Stir in the cornmeal, sugar, salt, spring onions and chilli. In a separate large bowl, beat together the eggs, yogurt and milk. Make a well in the centre of the dry ingredients and pour in the liquid ingredients. Stir gently until just combined; do not over-mix.

Spoon the mixture into the prepared muffin tin. Bake in the preheated oven for 15–20 minutes until well risen, golden brown and firm to the touch.

Leave the muffins in the tin for 5 minutes then serve warm or transfer to a wire rack and leave to cool.

Italian Tomato Muffins

makes 12

oil or melted butter, for greasing (if using)

140 g/5 oz plain flour

2 tbsp baking powder

½ tsp salt

200 g/7 oz fine polenta

1 egg, lightly beaten

300 ml/10 fl oz milk

300 g/10½ oz Italian plum tomatoes, peeled, deseeded and finely chopped

1 garlic clove, crushed

1 tbsp chopped fresh basil

1½ tsp chopped fresh parsley

Preheat the oven to 200°C/400°F/Gas Mark 6. Grease a 12-cup muffin tin or line with 12 paper cases.

Sift the flour, baking powder and salt into a large bowl. Add the polenta and mix well.

In a separate large bowl, whisk together the egg and milk. Add the tomatoes, garlic, basil and parsley and mix together. Make a well in the centre of the dry ingredients and pour in the liquid ingredients. Stir gently until just combined; do not over-mix.

Spoon the mixture into the prepared muffin tin. Bake in the preheated oven for 20 minutes until well risen, golden brown and firm to the touch.

Leave the muffins in the tin for 5 minutes then serve warm or transfer to a wire rack and leave to cool.

Mini Blue Cheese & Pear Muffins

makes 48

oil or melted butter,
for greasing (if using)

400 g/14 oz canned pear
halves in natural juice,
drained

280 g/10 oz plain flour

1 tbsp baking powder

pinch of salt

100 g/3½ oz blue cheese,
such as Stilton or Danish
Blue, finely crumbled

2 eggs

250 ml/9 fl oz milk

85 g/3 oz butter, melted
and cooled

40 g/1½ oz walnut pieces

pepper

Preheat the oven to 200°C/400°F/Gas Mark 6. Grease two 24-cup mini muffin tins or line with 48 mini paper cases. Chop the pears into small pieces. Sift together the flour, baking powder, salt and pepper to taste into a large bowl. Stir in the blue cheese and pears.

Lightly beat the eggs in a large bowl then beat in the milk and butter. Make a well in the centre of the dry ingredients and pour in the beaten liquid ingredients. Stir gently until just combined; do not over-mix.

Spoon the mixture into the prepared muffin tins. Scatter the walnuts over the tops of the muffins. Bake in the preheated oven for 15 minutes until well risen, golden brown and firm to the touch.

Leave the muffins in the tins for 5 minutes then serve warm or transfer to wire racks and leave to cool.

Smoked Salmon & Dill Muffins

makes 12

oil or melted butter, for greasing (if using)

280 g/10 oz plain flour

1 tbsp baking powder

pinch of salt

2 eggs

250 ml/9 fl oz buttermilk

85 g/3 oz butter, melted and cooled

150 g/5½ oz smoked salmon, finely chopped, plus extra to garnish

2 tbsp chopped fresh dill, plus extra sprigs to garnish

pepper

Preheat the oven to 200°C/400°F/Gas Mark 6. Grease a 12-cup muffin tin or line with 12 paper cases. Sift together the flour, baking powder, salt and pepper to taste into a large bowl.

Lightly beat the eggs in a large bowl then beat in the buttermilk and butter. Make a well in the centre of the dry ingredients, pour in the liquid ingredients and add the smoked salmon and dill. Stir gently until just combined; do not over-mix.

Spoon the mixture into the prepared muffin tin. Bake in the preheated oven for 20 minutes until well risen, golden brown and firm to the touch.

Leave the muffins in the tin for 5 minutes then serve warm or transfer to a wire rack and leave to cool. Serve garnished with small strips of smoked salmon and sprigs of dill.

Crab & Cream Cheese Muffins

makes 12

oil or melted butter, for greasing (if using)

280 g/10 oz plain flour

1½ tsp baking powder

½ tsp bicarbonate of soda

½ tsp salt

1 egg

150 ml/5 fl oz natural yogurt

150 ml/5 fl oz soured cream

25 g/1 oz Cheddar cheese, grated

25 g/1 oz fresh parsley, chopped

25 g/1 oz fresh dill, chopped

crab & cream cheese filling

200 g/7 oz canned crabmeat, drained

200 g/7 oz cream cheese

2 tbsp mayonnaise

salt and pepper

Preheat the oven to 200°C/400°F/Gas Mark 6. Grease a 12-cup muffin tin or line with 12 paper cases.

Sift the flour, baking powder, bicarbonate of soda and salt into a large bowl.

In a separate large bowl, lightly beat the egg, then pour in the yogurt and cream and mix together. Stir in the cheese and herbs. Make a well in the centre of the dry ingredients and pour in the liquid ingredients. Stir gently until just combined; do not over-mix.

Spoon the mixture into the prepared muffin tin. Bake in the preheated oven for 20 minutes until well risen, golden brown and firm to the touch.

Meanwhile, make the crab and cream cheese filling. Put the crabmeat in a large bowl and flake with a fork. Add the cream cheese and mayonnaise and mix together well. Season to taste with salt and pepper. Cover the bowl with clingfilm and chill in the refrigerator until ready for use.

Remove the muffins from the oven, leave in the tin for 5 minutes, then transfer to a wire rack and leave to cool. When cool, slice the muffins in half and fill with the crab and cream cheese filling.

Tuna & Olive Muffins

makes 12

oil or melted butter,
for greasing (if using)

90 g/3¼ oz stoned black
olives

280 g/10 oz plain flour

1 tbsp baking powder

pinch of salt

2 eggs

250 ml/9 fl oz buttermilk

85 g/3 oz butter, melted
and cooled

400 g/14 oz canned tuna
in olive oil, drained and
flaked

pepper

Preheat the oven to 200°C/400°F/Gas Mark 6. Grease a 12-cup muffin tin or line with 12 paper cases. Coarsely chop the olives, reserving 12 whole ones to garnish.

Sift together the flour, baking powder, salt and pepper to taste into a large bowl. Stir in the chopped olives.

Lightly beat the eggs in a large bowl then beat in the buttermilk and butter. Make a well in the centre of the dry ingredients, pour in the beaten liquid ingredients and add the tuna. Stir gently until just combined; do not over-mix.

Spoon the mixture into the prepared muffin tin. Top each muffin with one of the reserved olives. Bake in the preheated oven for 20 minutes until well risen, golden brown and firm to the touch.

Leave the muffins in the tins for 5 minutes then serve warm or transfer to wire racks and leave to cool.

Chicken & Sweetcorn Muffins

makes 12

oil or melted butter, for greasing (if using)

7 tbsp sunflower oil

1 onion, finely chopped

1 skinless chicken breast, about 175 g/6 oz, finely chopped

280 g/10 oz plain flour

1 tbsp baking powder

pinch of salt

2 eggs

250 ml/9 fl oz buttermilk

75 g/2¾ oz frozen sweetcorn kernels

pepper

paprika, to garnish

Preheat the oven to 200°C/400°F/Gas Mark 6. Grease a 12-cup muffin tin or line with 12 paper cases. Heat 1 tablespoon of the oil in a frying pan. Add the onion and cook for 2 minutes. Add the chicken and cook for 5 minutes, stirring occasionally, until tender. Remove from the heat and leave to cool.

Meanwhile, sift together the flour, baking powder, salt and pepper to taste into a large bowl.

Lightly beat the eggs in a large bowl then beat in the buttermilk and remaining oil. Make a well in the centre of the dry ingredients, pour in the beaten liquid ingredients and add the chicken mixture and sweetcorn. Stir gently until just combined; do not over-mix.

Spoon the mixture into the prepared muffin tin. Bake in the preheated oven for 20 minutes until well risen, golden brown and firm to the touch.

Leave the muffins in the tin for 5 minutes, sprinkle with paprika and serve warm or transfer to a wire rack and leave to cool.

Spicy Chicken Muffins

makes 12

oil or melted butter,
for greasing (if using)

125 ml/4 fl oz vegetable oil

2 onions, chopped

3 spring onions, chopped

1 small fresh red chilli,
deseeded and finely
chopped

3 skinless, boneless
chicken thighs, chopped

1 tsp paprika

315 g/11 oz self-raising
flour

1 tsp baking powder

2 eggs

1 tbsp lemon juice

1 tbsp grated lemon rind

125 ml/4 fl oz soured cream

125 ml/4 fl oz
natural yogurt

Preheat the oven to 190°C/375°F/Gas Mark 5. Grease a 12-cup muffin tin or line with 12 paper cases.

Heat a little of the oil in a frying pan, add the onions, spring onions and chilli and cook, stirring constantly, for 3 minutes. Remove from the heat, lift out the onions and chilli and leave to cool. Heat a little more oil in the frying pan, add the chicken and paprika, and cook, stirring, for 5 minutes. Remove from the heat and set aside.

Meanwhile, sift together the flour and baking powder into a large bowl. In a separate large bowl, lightly beat the eggs, then stir in the remaining oil and the lemon juice and rind. Pour in the soured cream and yogurt and mix together. Make a well in the centre of the dry ingredients and pour in the beaten liquid ingredients, then gently stir in the onions, spring onion mixture and chicken until just combined; do not over-mix.

Spoon the mixture into the prepared muffin tin. Bake in the preheated oven for 20 minutes until well risen, golden brown and firm to the touch.

Leave the muffins in the tin for 5 minutes then serve warm or transfer to a wire rack and leave to cool.

Cheese & Ham Muffins

makes 12

oil or melted butter,
for greasing (if using)

280 g/10 oz plain flour

1 tbsp baking powder

pinch of salt

100 g/3½ oz sliced ham,
finely chopped

140 g/5 oz mature Cheddar
cheese, coarsely grated

2 eggs

250 ml/9 fl oz milk

85 g/3 oz butter, melted
and cooled

pepper

Preheat the oven to 200°C/400°F/Gas Mark 6. Grease a 12-cup muffin tin or line with 12 paper cases. Sift together the flour, baking powder, salt and pepper to taste into a large bowl. Stir in the ham and 100 g/3½ oz of the cheese.

Lightly beat the eggs in a large bowl then beat in the milk and butter. Make a well in the centre of the dry ingredients and pour in the beaten liquid ingredients. Stir gently until just combined; do not over-mix.

Spoon the mixture into the prepared muffin tin. Scatter the remaining cheese over the tops of the muffins. Bake in the preheated oven for 20 minutes until well risen, golden brown and firm to the touch.

Leave the muffins in the tin for 5 minutes then serve warm or transfer to a wire rack and leave to cool.

Savoury Leek & Ham Muffins

makes 12

oil or melted butter,
for greasing (if using)

2 tbsp vegetable oil

1 leek, trimmed and finely
chopped

280 g/10 oz plain flour

2 tsp baking powder

½ tsp bicarbonate of soda

1 egg, lightly beaten

300 ml/10 fl oz thick
natural yogurt

55 g/2 oz butter, melted
and cooled

25 g/1 oz Cheddar cheese,
grated

25 g/1 oz fresh chives,
finely snipped

150 g/5½ oz cooked ham,
chopped

Preheat the oven to 200°C/400°F/Gas Mark 6. Grease a 12-cup muffin tin or line with 12 paper cases.

Heat the oil in a frying pan, add the leek, and cook, stirring, for 2 minutes. Remove from the heat and leave to cool.

Meanwhile, sift together the flour, baking powder and bicarbonate of soda into a large bowl. In a separate large bowl, lightly mix together the egg, yogurt and butter. Add the cheese, chives, cooked leek and half of the ham, then mix together well. Make a well in the centre of the dry ingredients and pour in the liquid ingredients. Stir gently until just combined; do not over-mix.

Spoon the mixture into the prepared muffin tin and sprinkle over the remaining ham. Bake in the preheated oven for 20 minutes until well risen, golden brown and firm to the touch.

Leave the muffins in the tin for 5 minutes then serve warm or transfer to a wire rack and leave to cool.

Spicy Chorizo Muffins

makes 12

oil or melted butter, for greasing (if using)

280 g/10 oz plain flour

1 tbsp baking powder

pinch of salt

1 tsp ground paprika, plus extra to garnish

100 g/3½ oz chorizo sausage, outer casing removed, finely chopped

1 small red pepper, cored, deseeded and finely chopped

2 eggs

250 ml/9 fl oz buttermilk

85 g/3 oz butter, melted and cooled

1 garlic clove, crushed

Preheat the oven to 200°C/400°F/Gas Mark 6. Grease a 12-cup muffin tin or line with 12 paper cases. Sift together the flour, baking powder, salt and taste into a large bowl. Stir in the sausage and red pepper.

Lightly beat the eggs in a large bowl then beat in the buttermilk, butter and garlic. Make a well in the centre of the dry ingredients and pour in the beaten liquid ingredients. Stir gently until just combined; do not over-mix.

Spoon the mixture into the prepared muffin tin. Bake in the preheated oven for 20 minutes until well risen, golden brown and firm to the touch.

Leave the muffins in the tin for 5 minutes, sprinkle with paprika then serve warm or transfer to a wire rack and leave to cool.